Inference
Reading Comprehension Book
Reading Level 2.0–3.5

Introduction

Welcome to the Edupress Inference Reading Comprehension Book. This resource is an effective tool for instruction, practice, and evaluation of student understanding of how to make inferences. It includes ideas on how to introduce inferring to students, as well as activities to help teach and practice the concept.

The reproducible activities in this book are tailored to individual, small-group, and whole-class work. They include leveled reading passages, graphic organizers, worksheets, and detailed instruction pages. These activities provide opportunities to use text, illustrations, graphics, and combinations of these elements to practice making inferences from text.

The material in this book is written for readers at the 2.0–3.5 reading level. However, the activities can easily be adapted to your students' ability levels and your time frame. After introducing an activity to students, model it by working through one or two examples aloud. You may wish to also read text passages aloud to students, or they can be read silently or aloud by students. For students who need personalized help, individual and small-group activities have been included. These activities can be done alone or with a classroom aide for explicit instruction.

We know you will be pleased with the progress your students make in being able to infer ideas from text after using this book.

EP2360 © 2010 GHC Specialty Brands, LLC • 401 S. Wright Road • Janesville, WI 53547
ISBN 13: 978-1-56472-148-8
www.edupressinc.com

Table of Contents

Directions: Introducing Inference

Whole Class ●●●

Introduce the idea of using inference while reading. Explain that when readers make inferences, they takes clues from the text and/or pictures, add the clues to what they already know, and come up with ideas the author does not directly state. Read a short picture book such as *Officer Buckle and Gloria* by Peggy Rathmann. Pause after reading about Officer Buckle's first speech at Napville School. Model making an inference. For example, "The text says nobody listened to Officer Buckle and there was snoring. In the picture, students are making paper airplanes, doing puzzles, and napping during Officer Buckle's talk. I know when I feel bored, I don't pay close attention to the speaker. So even though the author does not directly say the students feel bored, those actions give me the idea that the students feel bored."

Continue reading the story. Pause after a few pages, and guide students in making an inference. Draw and label an inference graphic organizer on the board similar to the "Sister Skate" Graphic Organizer on page 5. Think aloud, "I wonder how the children in the audience feel now?" Ask students what clues in the text and picture can help them know how the children feel. Record their answers in the graphic organizer. Have students think about a time when they used the same actions. Ask how they felt at the time and record their answers in the organizer. Review the clues and the students' prior knowledge and ask, "How do the children feel now?" Record the answer. Continue reading, pausing several times to guide students through making inferences.

Whole Class/Individual ●●●/○

Reproduce "Sister Skate" on page 4 and the graphic organizer on page 5 for each student. Explain that sometimes readers only have clues from the text and what they already know to make inferences. Read the story aloud. Then, read the directions, questions, and labels on the graphic organizer aloud. Explain that the organizer will help the students make inferences to answer the questions. Reread the first question. Have students find clues in the text to help them fill in the first box. Then, have students record what they already know about the clues in the second box. Finally, instruct students to use what they wrote in the first two boxes to make an inference that answers the question and to write the answer in the third box. Have students continue the process independently until each question is completed.

When all students have finished, discuss the answers to the questions as a class. As an extension, ask students to explain how to make an inference in three simple steps.

Answer Key

"Sister Skate" Graphic Organizer, suggested answers (Page 5)

1. She holds a cup of hot chocolate to keep her hands warm. Maggie skates on ice. + prior knowledge will vary = Annie wears a sweater because it is cold at the rink.

2. Annie did not watch Maggie lace her skates. She was too busy looking at the extra bag. + prior knowledge will vary = Annie was so distracted by the extra bag that she did not drink her hot chocolate.

3. "You need to carry your own skates if you are going to be a skater." Annie smiled and grabbed both bags. + prior knowledge will vary = Annie does want to skate next week.

Sister Skate

Annie ran back to her room and pulled on a sweater. It was time to go to the ice rink. Annie loved spending time at the rink. She would sit with her mother on the bench while her big sister, Maggie, skated. Her mother always bought her hot chocolate. Holding the cup helped keep her hands warm. She would sip her drink as she watched Maggie skate. By the time Annie drank the last drop, it was time to go home.

"Let's go, girls. We don't want to miss the bus," Mom said.

The bus pulled up to the curb just as they reached the bus stop. Annie, Maggie, and Mom sat on the long seat. Annie turned around and looked out the window as they passed the park. The trees were covered in snow. They sparkled in the sunlight. When the bus stopped, Annie followed her mother off the bus. The bus driver called out, "Have fun, girls!"

Maggie said, "Thank you, Maria. You have a good day too!"

As they walked toward the rink, Annie saw Maggie was carrying two bags. "Why do you have two bags instead of one?" Annie asked.

Maggie grinned. "That's for me to know and for you to find out," she said.

Annie frowned. Maggie always liked keeping secrets from her. "I don't care about what you have in the bag!" Annie said.

Mom went to buy the hot chocolate while Annie and Maggie went to their regular bench. Maggie said, "Watch how I lace my skates."

Annie did not watch Maggie lace her skates. She was too busy looking at the extra bag. Maggie went onto the ice when their mother got to the bench. Annie did not sip her hot chocolate. She did not watch her sister glide and spin on the ice. Instead, Annie stared at the extra bag. Her drink went from hot to warm to cool. Finally, Maggie came off the ice. "Are you ready for your surprise?" Maggie asked. She opened the extra bag and pulled out another pair of skates. "I think these will fit you," she said. "I'll lace them for you so you can know how they should feel."

A smile lit up Annie's face. After she put the skates on, Annie inched her way onto the ice with her sister. She squeezed Maggie's hand and held on tight. She listened carefully to Maggie's directions. Before long, the sisters were skating together.

When they were ready to go home, Maggie handed Annie the extra bag. Maggie said, "You need to carry your own skates, if you are going to be a skater. We can do another sister skate next week after I practice."

Annie smiled and grabbed both bags. "I'll even carry your skates!" she said.

"Sister Skate" Graphic Organizer

Directions: Fill in the boxes to answer each question.

Why does Annie wear a sweater to the rink?

The story tells me:
_____
_____
_____
_____

+

I know:
_____
_____
_____

=

So I think:
_____
_____
_____
_____

Why didn't Annie drink her hot chocolate?

The story tells me:
_____
_____
_____
_____

+

I know:
_____
_____
_____

=

So I think:
_____
_____
_____
_____

Does Annie want to skate next week?

The story tells me:
_____
_____
_____

+

I know:
_____
_____
_____

=

So I think:
_____
_____
_____
_____

Directions: Picture Inference

Individual ●

Reproduce Why Is the Boy Crying? and Why Is the Boy Smiling? on pages 7 and 8 for each student. Remind students that a reader sometimes uses clues in pictures to better understand what is happening. Direct the students' attention to the first illustration. Think aloud, "I see the boy is crying. He is alone in a grocery store. The shelves are taller than him. I saw a boy crying in a store once. He couldn't find his mother. He cried because he felt afraid. I think the boy in the picture is crying because he is afraid."

Ask students, "Have you ever cried in a grocery store? Why? What were you feeling? Why do you think the boy in the picture is crying?" Have students use what they see in the pictures and what they already know to answer the question on the lines provided. For additional practice, have students continue with Why Is the Boy Smiling?

Collect and review the papers, looking for responses that clearly answer each question and reflect the clues in the illustration. Review the inference process and have students revise their answers, if necessary.

Small Group ●●

Reproduce Draw Your Own Inference Picture on page 9 for each student. Ask students to think about a time they laughed. Where were they? Who were they with? What were they doing? Have students draw the scene in the blank box. Next, have students write a paragraph on the lines below the picture describing the scene. Remind students that the pictures should contain clues to why they are laughing.

Afterward, have students fold their papers in half so only the drawing is showing. Have each student trade pictures with a partner. On a separate sheet of paper, partners should write a paragraph describing the scene and explaining why the person in the drawing is laughing. Then, have students share and compare the paragraphs and discuss why they are alike or different. Ask students what clues in their partner's pictures helped them answer the question.

Whole Class ●●●

Reproduce two copies each of Why Is the Boy Crying? and Why Is the Boy Smiling? on heavy paper. Cut the illustrations apart, and spread the cards faceup in two piles on a table in front of the class. You may also wish to include copies of photos from newspapers and magazines that show people expressing emotions. On the board, draw five columns. Label the columns: happy, sad, angry, afraid, and proud. Repeat the process on the other side of the board. Divide the class into two teams. Tell students to think about why the boy in the picture is crying or smiling. Have one member from each team come forward, select a picture, and tape it in the correct column. When the team member returns to the end of the line, the next player takes a turn. Explain that players need to find clues in the pictures and think about what they already know to decide what the boy in the picture is feeling. After teams finish, have them explain their choices to the class. The team with the most correct choices is the winner.

Why Is the Boy Crying?

Name:_____

Directions: Study each picture. Then answer the question, "Why is the boy crying?" on the lines next to each picture.

Why Is the Boy Smiling?

Directions: Study each picture. Then answer the question, "Why is the boy smiling?" on the lines next to each picture.

Draw Your Own Inference Picture

Name:_____

Directions: Think about a time you laughed. Where were you? What were you doing? Draw a picture of what happened. Then write four or five sentences telling why you laughed.

Why is _____ **laughing?**

Directions: Inference Charades

Individual ●

Reproduce one set of Occupation Cards and one set of Animal Cards on pages 11 and 12. Cut the cards apart and place them in a paper bag. Have each student pull one card from the bag. Then, have students write a paragraph describing the animal or occupation they chose without ever using the word or words on the card. Review paragraphs for descriptive details.

Small Group ●●

Divide the class into groups of three or four students. Have students take turns reading the paragraphs they wrote in the Individual activity. After each paragraph is read, the other members of the group should guess what animal or occupation the paragraph describes.

Have students explain their guesses. What clues did they find in the paragraph? What did they already know that helped them determine the answer?

Whole Class ●●●

Reproduce one set of Occupation Cards. Cut the cards apart and place them in a paper bag. Choose one student to pull a card from the bag and act out the occupation. The rest of the class should guess the occupation. The student who correctly names the occupation first should explain to the class how he or she determined the answer. Then, that student should draw a new card and act out the occupation on the card.

Instead of acting out the occupation, the student can give verbal clues to the class, describing the occupation. In this format, explain that students must not use the words on the card when giving clues. Reproduce the animal cards for additional practice. Have students describe in detail the process they used to determine their answers.

Occupation Cards

clown	fireman	house painter	police officer
teacher	cook	writer	farmer
doctor	mail carrier	zoo keeper	artist
bank teller	singer	dancer	bus driver
dentist	house builder	nurse	librarian

Animal Cards

bear	cow	dog	duck
horse	lamb	cat	monkey
pig	rabbit	elephant	turtle
chicken	parrot	deer	donkey
fox	lion	owl	raccoon

Directions: Who? What? Where?

Individual

Read one or two of the riddles from the Who? What? Where? Riddles page on page 14 to the class. Point out the kinds of clues found in the riddles. "The clues about the kite describe what a kite looks like and what a kite does. The question, 'What am I?' tells us it is a thing."

Draw four lines on the board. Think aloud, "I am going to write a riddle about a clock. What does a clock look like? It has numbers on its face." Write the clue on the first line. Think aloud, "Some clocks have hands, but some don't. I'll write, 'Sometimes I have hands.'" Record the clue. Think aloud, "What does a clock do? When I look at it, it tells me what time it is." Write the clue on the third line. ("I can't talk, but I can tell you what time it is.") On the last line, write, "What am I?" as you think aloud, "I know this is a thing so I will start my question with the word, 'What.'" Repeat the process with another person, place, or thing. Have students suggest the clues.

Reproduce the Make Your Own Riddle worksheet on page 15 for each student. Have students work independently to write three new riddles. Have students write the answers to their riddles on the back of the worksheet. Collect and review the papers. Check to make sure the clues are focused and the answer can be inferred. Pass the papers back and have students trade with a partner. Have partners write their guesses on the space provided. Then, have them check each other's work.

Small Group

Reproduce Who? What? Where? Riddles on page 14 for each student. Read the first riddle to the class. Ask what clues help them figure out the answer. Ask if anything they already knew helped them figure out the answer. Divide the class into pairs. Have student pairs work together to answer the riddles.

Whole Class

Divide the class into two teams. Use the students' original riddles from the Individual exercise, or provide a set of riddles for a game of Who? What? Where? Have one student read a riddle to the class. The first person to answer correctly earns a point for his or her team. Continue until each student has had an opportunity to read a riddle aloud. Have students explain how they determined their answers.

Answer Key

Who? What? Where? Riddles (Page 14)

1. kite
2. George Washington
3. circus
4. train
5. Johnny Appleseed
6. Plymouth Rock
7. birthday cake
8. Betsy Ross
9. library
10. penny

Who? What? Where? Riddles

Name:_____

Directions: Read each riddle. Write the answer on the line below the riddle.

1 I have a tail.
I fly in the sky.
I come in many shapes
    and colors.
What am I?

_____

2 I was the first person to
    have my job.
I cannot tell a lie.
I am the father of our country.
Who am I?

_____

3 I am in a big tent.
I see a man in a top hat.
I see animals and clowns in rings.
Where am I?

_____

4 I am always on track.
I carry people and things.
I am made of many cars.
What am I?

_____

5 My real name is John Chapman.
I visited many places in the
    United States long ago.
I gave people apple trees
    and seeds to plant.
Who am I?

_____

6 I am at a famous place.
I can look out at the water.
Long ago, the Mayflower
    landed here.
Where am I?

_____

7 I am sweet!
People sing when they see me.
You can count my candles.
What am I?

_____

8 I was born on January 1, 1752.
I won a sewing contest when
    I was young.
Many people think I made
    the first U.S. flag.
Who am I?

_____

9 I look for free adventures here.
I get lost between the stacks.
I like to check out the books.
Where am I?

_____

10 I am flat and round.
My face looks like Abe Lincoln.
Having me in your pocket
    makes cents.
What am I?

_____

Make Your Own Riddle

Name:_____

Directions: Think about a person, place, or thing. Write the clues on the lines. Then, write the answer on the back of the page.

CLUES _____
_____
_____
_____
_____

What am I? _____

CLUES _____
_____
_____
_____
_____

Who am I? _____

CLUES _____
_____
_____
_____

Where am I? _____

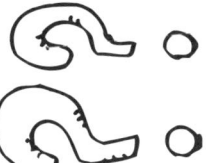

   15

Directions: Using Clue Words

Individual

Write the words "fish," "beach," and "summer" on the board. Draw a picture of a lake with fish jumping, the sun shining, someone on the beach with a fishing pole, and someone in a rowboat with a fishing pole. Think aloud, "When I look at my picture, I see some things like the fish and the beach are clue words. But some other things, like the sun and the fisherman, are things I inferred. I put together the clue words and what I already know about the lake and came up with a new idea." Ask the students to find something else in the picture that shows you put the clues together with what you already knew.

Reproduce Read, Think, Draw! 1 on page 17 for each student. Read the directions with the class. Then, have students complete the drawings and questions independently.

Collect and review the papers. Look for evidence the student understands the difference between what is directly stated and what is inferred. Also, evaluate the student's ability to make a reasonable inference.

Small Group

Divide the class into groups of three or four students. Reproduce Read, Think, Draw! 2 on page 18 for each student. Distribute the pages and have the students use the first set of clues to draw a picture and answer the questions. When they finish, have students share their pictures and discuss the questions with the members of the group.

Next, have each student read the second set of clues and draw the picture. Then, have each student trade papers with someone in his or her group and answer the questions based on that drawing. When completed, students should share the picture with the group and explain their answers.

Collect and review the papers. Check to make sure the answers reflect an understanding of the difference between directly stated and inferred information. Listen to the students' explanations of their answers.

Whole Class

Divide the class into three or four groups. Provide each group with a Read, Think, Draw! page, a piece of poster board, pencils, and crayons or markers. Have students work together within their group to read the clues and draw the setting. When finished, display the drawings. Read the questions to the class, and discuss each drawing as a class.

Listen for evidence that students understand the difference between directly stated information and inferred information. Ask students to explain how they made an inference.

Read, Think, Draw! 1

Name:_____

Directions: Read the clue words. Use the words to draw a picture of the setting. Then look at your picture and answer the questions.

CLUE WORDS:
swing
grass
children

Which things in your picture are clue words?

_____

Which things show you used the clues and what you already knew?

_____

CLUE WORDS:
summer
swim
family

Which things in your picture are clue words?

_____

Which things show you used the clues and what you already knew?

_____

Read, Think, Draw! 2

Name:_____

Directions: Read the clue words. Use the words to draw a picture of the setting. Then, look at your picture and answer the questions.

CLUE WORDS:

game

field

team

Which things in your picture are clue words?

_____

Which things show you used the clues and what you already knew?

_____

CLUE WORDS:

winter

play

snow

Which things in your picture are clue words?

_____

Which things show you used the clues and what you already knew?

_____

Directions: I See, Therefore, I Think

Individual

Reproduce I See, I Think 1 and 2 on pages 20 and 21 for each student. Distribute the pages, and then draw the students' attention to the first illustration. On the board, write the following sentences, "There is a boy, a girl, a man, and a woman. There is a family." Think aloud, "When I look at the picture, I see a boy, a girl, a man, and a woman. I think they are a family because there are adults and children together and they remind me of families I know." Next, write the following sentences on the board, "The people are carrying backpacks and suitcases. There are airplanes. They are in an airport. The family is taking a trip." Ask the students which sentences are things they see in the picture. Ask students which sentences show new ideas inferred from the pictures. Then, have students complete the other examples independently.

Collect and review the papers. Sentences should clearly show an understanding of the difference between what is directly pictured and what is inferred.

Small Group

Have each student draw a picture of an event from real life or a story he or she has read. Next, have each student trade pictures with a partner. Each partner should write two sentences about the picture. The first sentence should be about things the student sees in his or her partner's picture. The second sentence should be about things the student infers from his or her partner's picture. When finished, one student should read the sentences aloud to the partner. The partner states whether the sentence is an "I See" or an "I Think" sentence. The students then discuss the answers and reverse roles.

When all students have finished, collect and review the papers. Check to make sure the answers reflect an understanding of the difference between what is pictured and what is inferred.

Whole Class

Prior to class, reproduce the illustrations on transparencies. On index cards, write two or three observations and two or three inferences about each illustration, one per card. Put all of the cards for each illustration into four separate paper bags.

Divide the class into two teams. Display the first illustration on the overhead, and pull a card from the coordinating bag. Read the sentence aloud, and state whether the sentence says something you see in the picture or an idea you get from the picture. Explain your answer. Have a student from the first team pull another card from the bag, read the sentence, state whether the sentence tells something he/she sees in the picture or an idea that comes from the picture, and explain his/her answer. Repeat the process with a member of the other team and a new card. Rotate between teams, and award a point for each correct answer. Adjust the number of sentence cards so each member of the class has an opportunity to participate.

Listen for evidence that the students understand the difference between observation and inference.

I See, I Think 1

Directions: Look at the pictures. Under each picture, write a sentence telling what you see in the picture. Then, write a sentence telling things you infer from the picture.

I see ➤ _____

_____

I think ➤ _____

_____

I see ➤ _____

_____

I think ➤ _____

_____

I See, I Think 2

Directions: Look at the pictures. Under each picture, write a sentence telling what you see in the picture. Then, write a sentence telling things you infer from the picture.

I see ➤ _____

_____

I think ➤ _____

_____

I see ➤ _____

_____

I think ➤ _____

_____

   21

Directions: Inferring Feelings

Individual ●

Reproduce How Do I Feel? 1 and 2 on pages 23 and 24 for each student. Have students read the passages independently and use the word bank to answer the questions that follow on the lines provided. Remind students to use clues in the story and prior knowledge to come up with the correct answer. Then, discuss the activity as a class.

Small Group ● ●

Divide the class into groups of three or four students. Reproduce and distribute one page of the How Do I Feel? pages. Have the students read the passages and discuss the answers within their group. Next, have each student write a paragraph. Remind students the paragraph should show but not tell how the character in the story feels. At the bottom of the paper, the student should write how the character feels. Have each student read the paragraph, but not the answer, to the group. The other members of the group listen to the story and determine how the character feels.

Collect and review the papers. Check to make sure the answers can be inferred from the information in the paragraph. Listen to the group discussions.

Whole Class ● ● ●

Write the following words on the board: happy, sad, angry, afraid, surprised, and sleepy. Read aloud the passages on the How Do I Feel? pages. After each passage, ask students how the main character feels. Have students explain their answers. Tape the passage under the feeling word it describes.

Next, divide the class into two teams and have students write a paragraph that shows, but does not tell, how their characters feel (happy, sad, angry, afraid, surprised, or sleepy). Have each team write on different colored paper. Post a set of the target feeling words in two separate areas of the classroom. Collect the paragraphs, and trade them with the opposing teams. Have team members take turns reading the paragraphs. As a team, members should decide which feeling is expressed in the paragraph and post the paragraph under the correct label. Play stops when a team has posted all of their paragraphs. Review the answers and discuss as a class. The first team to correctly sort the paragraphs and explain their answers wins.

Listen to the students' answers and explanations for evidence of their understanding of the inference process and their ability to apply the process to the written word.

Answer Key

How Do I Feel? 1 (Page 23)	How Do I Feel? 2 (Page 24)
1. sleepy	1. angry
2. sad	2. happy
3. surprised	3. afraid

How Do I Feel? 1

Directions: Read each story. Use a feeling from the word bank to answer each question.

Mary looked out the window at the full moon. Then, she looked back at her book and flipped the pages to the end of the chapter. "Only two more pages," she thought. She tried to read, but the lines ran together. She put the book down and rubbed her eyes. She opened her book again and read the first sentence. A yawn forced her mouth to open wide. She wondered if she would make it to the end of the chapter.

How does Mary feel? _____

Tim reached for the end of the string, but it slipped out of his hand. His mother ran out into the yard to help him, but it was too late. They watched the red balloon sail up into the sky. Tim hung his head and slowly went into the house. He went right to his room and climbed into his bed. He buried his face in his pillow. Mama could hear Tim sniffling quietly.

How does Tim feel? _____

The forest was much quieter than the city. Luis and his father walked along the path. The only sound came from the twigs snapping under their feet. Luis watched the path carefully. As he turned a bend, a squirrel bolted out from under a bush and crossed the path just inches from Luis's foot. Luis shrieked and jumped backward. He backed into his father and tumbled to the ground. They both laughed as the squirrel disappeared into the grass.

How does Luis feel? _____

happy	angry	surprised
sad	afraid	sleepy

How Do I Feel? 2

Directions: Read each story. Use a feeling from the word bank to answer each question.

Meg rubbed and rubbed the white drawing board. On TV, the board always came clean with one quick wipe. Meg looked at the shadows of the colors covering her board. No matter how much she rubbed the board, it would not come clean. Meg pressed her lips together and took a deep breath through her nose. Finally, she threw the toy in the trash and slammed her door. She planted her hands on her hips and stamped her foot. That cost a whole month of savings, Meg thought. Things never really work like they do on TV.

How does Meg feel? _____

Cam pulled on his baseball cap and grabbed his glove. He ran out onto the front porch to wait for Grandfather. Today was opening day at the ballpark. Grandfather had said their seats were almost on the field. Cam hoped he would catch a foul ball. Cam looked up at the sun and smiled. This was a perfect day for watching a baseball game.

How does Cam feel? _____

The thunder shook the house. The lightning split the sky. Then, the lights went out. James pulled a small flashlight from his pocket. Jazmin followed her brother and the bobbing light through the black-as-coal hallway. In the dark, strange sounds filled the house. Goose-bumps covered Jazmin's arms. A gust of wind howled through the trees and caused something to crash against the house. Jazmin gasped and grabbed her brother's arm.

How does Jazmin feel? _____

| happy | angry | surprised |
| sad | afraid | sleepy |

Directions: Inferring Action

Individual ●

Reproduce What Am I Doing? 1 and 2 on pages 26 and 27 for each student. Have students read each passage independently and answer the question that follows. Remind students to use clues in the story and prior knowledge to come up with the correct answer. Then, have them draw a picture in each box of the action described. Discuss the activity as a class when all students are finished. What words helped them determine the answers?

Small Group ● ●

Divide the class into groups of four students. Reproduce What Am I Doing? 1 or 2 for each group. Cut the passages out and place them facedown in the center of each group. Have students work in pairs to read and act out the passages. Explain that while one partner is reading the words, the other partner will become a "living picture" by completing the actions described. The other group members will then try to guess the activity. After the group finishes all of the passages, they should discuss how both the words and the actions helped them determine the correct answer.

Whole Class ● ● ●

Draw a flowchart on the board. Place three open squares in a column and one open square to the right of the column. Draw an arrow from the column to the square on the right. Read aloud the first passage and question on What Am I Doing? 1. Ask a student to tell one clue in the description that will help the class answer the question, "What am I doing?" Record the answer in the first box in the left column. Continue until the entire left column is filled. Then ask a student what answer would be supported by those clues. Record the answer in the box on the right. Repeat the process with the second passage.

Next, divide the class into teams of four students. Have each team draw a flowchart on the board and line up in front of their chart. Explain that after you read a passage aloud, the first three students in line will go to the board one at a time and fill in a clue box, and the last student will use the clues to help them answer the question, "What am I doing?" The first team to correctly complete the chart wins a point. Continue play with the passages on What Am I Doing? 2 or passages from grade-level books. Have students rotate line positions, so each student has an opportunity to answer the question.

Look at the flowcharts for evidence of students' understanding of the inference process and their ability to apply the process to the written word.

Answer Key

What Am I Doing? 1 (Page 26)

1. riding a bike
2. putting together a jigsaw puzzle
3. eating an ice cream cone

What Am I Doing? 2 (Page 27)

1. playing basketball
2. reading a book
3. making a bed

What Am I Doing? 1

Name:_____

Directions: Read each paragraph. Draw lines under the words in the story that help you answer the question. Then, write your answer on the line and draw a picture of the action in the box provided.

I toss my book into the basket. I grab the handles. I lift one leg up and swing it over to the other side. I sit back on the seat and lift one foot off the ground. Then, I start to roll forward a bit. Next, I lift my other foot off the ground. I feel a little wobbly at first. My right knee goes up as my left knee goes down. Up and down they go as I pump the pedals, and I am soon moving fast and steady. Before long, I will be home.

What am I doing? _____

I want to sort the pieces by shape, but my sister wants to sort by color. We both agree to work from the outside in. I start on the bottom of the frame, while my sister starts at the top. I lift a piece and study it. It has one flat, smooth side. It looks like a piece of the grass. I think it is part of the bottom of the frame. I try to fit it into one spot, then another, but it does not work. I almost give up, but then I see another piece on the table. It is the same color as the piece in my hand. It looks the right shape to connect to the piece I am holding. I try to connect the pieces together. They fit! Only 498 more pieces to go!

What are we doing? _____

I wrap a napkin around the bottom to catch the drips. I take my first lick. I want to take a big bite, but I know if I go too fast it will make my head hurt. I take lick after lick, working all the way around the cold surface. When I reach the holder, I stop to wipe my chin. I notice some of it has dripped onto my shirt. I take a bite and enjoy the mix of crunchy and creamy.

What am I doing? _____

What Am I Doing? 2

Directions: Read each paragraph. Draw lines under the words in the story that help you answer the question. Then, write your answer on the line and draw a picture of the action in the box provided.

I push the orange rubber down towards the floor. It bounces back to the palm of my hand. I dribble down the court and stop in a clearing. I bend my knees and then straighten my legs and reach my hands high. I feel the bumpy rubber roll off my fingertips. I watch it soar up and land on a metal rim. It dances around the rim for a minute and then falls through the net.

What am I doing? _____

I sit in my favorite chair and open the cover. I can hear its spine crack. I read the title and flip forward a few pages. I look at the picture at the top of the page and the words below it. Before long, I can picture myself riding on a pirate ship. I turn page after page until it is time for dinner. I place an unused postcard between the pages to mark my place. Then, I close the cover.

What am I doing? _____

I always begin my day with this chore. First, I pull the soft sheet up and smooth out the wrinkles with my hand. Next, I pull the thick blanket up over the sheet, smooth that out too, and then tuck in the ends. Then, I fluff my pillows and put them in place. Now, I'm almost finished with my chore.

What am I doing? _____

Directions: Inferring Feelings Through Dialogue

Individual ●

Reproduce How Am I Feeling? Quotes on page 29 for each student. Have students read the quotations independently and draw a line between the quotation and the word that matches the feeling the quotation shows. Remind students to read the quote and think about when and why they might say something like it. When all students have finished, discuss the answers as a class.

Small Group ● ●

Reproduce How Am I Feeling? Quotes for each student. Have students complete the sheet independently and then find a partner. Explain that good readers also use inference when listening or reading text out loud. Write the following sentence on the board: "The phone call is for me." Read the sentence aloud as if you were excited about the phone call. Ask students how you felt. Then, read the same sentence aloud as if you are surprised the call is for you. Ask students to identify this second emotion. Then, have partners take turns reading the quotations

with the emotions they matched to it. As one partner reads, the other partner should listen and check to make sure the sentence/emotion combination makes sense.

Whole Class

Divide the class into two teams. Copy the emotion words on page 29 on pieces of paper, one word per page, written large enough to be read from a distance. Have each member of the team hold at least one card. (Create additional emotion cards if necessary.) Read the first quotation to the class, and tell students to raise the word card if it matches the emotion shown in the quotation. Award a team one point for every correct response. Provide more quotations from books the class has read for more practice. The team with the most points at the end wins.

Discuss both correct and incorrect responses. Ask students to explain their answers.

Answer Key

How Am I Feeling? Quotes (Page 29)

1. sad
2. angry
3. afraid
4. surprised
5. sleepy

6. shy
7. hungry
8. excited
9. proud
10. lonely

How Am I Feeling? Quotes

Name:_____

Directions: Draw a line between the sentence and the feeling it shows. Use each word once.

① "This movie makes me cry."

② "I won't play anymore if you won't play by the rules."

③ "I am not going in the cave because it is too dark in there."

④ "I never thought I would see you here!"

⑤ "I can't stop yawning."

⑥ "It is hard for me talk around people I don't know."

⑦ "I could eat five sandwiches right now!"

⑧ "Wow! I'm going on a safari!"

⑨ "I earned a blue ribbon for my science project!"

⑩ "Everyone is too busy to talk to or play with me."

afraid

angry

excited

hungry

lonely

proud

sad

shy

sleepy

surprised

Directions: Describing Places

Individual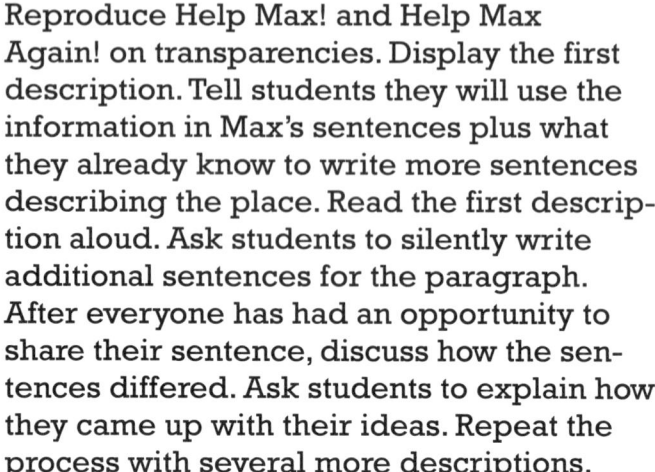

Reproduce Help Max! and Help Max Again! on pages 31 and 32 for each student. Read the directions with the class. Then, have students independently read each description of a place Max visited and write two more sentences describing the place. Remind students to use Max's sentences as well as what they already know about each place to help them write their own sentences. Have volunteers read their sentences to the class.

Small Group

Divide the class into pairs. Reproduce Help Max! for each pair of students. Read the directions with the class. Then, have one member of each pair read Max's description of a place. Each student adds a sentence to the description and explains what clues in the text or prior knowledge helped him or her decide what to write. Students take turns reading until each description is completed. Hold a class discussion when the activity is complete. Listen to the students' justifications of their answers.

Whole Class

Reproduce Help Max! and Help Max Again! on transparencies. Display the first description. Tell students they will use the information in Max's sentences plus what they already know to write more sentences describing the place. Read the first description aloud. Ask students to silently write additional sentences for the paragraph. After everyone has had an opportunity to share their sentence, discuss how the sentences differed. Ask students to explain how they came up with their ideas. Repeat the process with several more descriptions.

Help Max!

Directions: Max went to many places this year. He wants to describe all of them. Help Max finish his work. Read each paragraph. Then, write two more sentences describing the place. Use what Max tells you and what you already know to write the new sentences.

1 **I went to a farm in the spring. The farmer raises animals. A big red barn was behind the house. Next to it, there was a chicken coop.**

_____

_____

2 **I visited the new library! The first thing I saw was a very long desk. People holding books stood in line in front of the desk. I saw a big sign with "Children's Room" written on it. I went to the area and saw bookcases and all kinds of things to sit on.**

_____

_____

3 **I went to a big city in the summer. The streets were very busy. There were many people walking or riding somewhere. Tall buildings with big windows lined the streets.**

_____

_____

4 **I went to the county fair in the summer. I saw the Ferris wheel from the parking lot! There was a map by the front gate. It showed us where we could find the games, rides, shows, and food stands.**

_____

_____

Help Max Again!

Name:_____

Directions: Max went to many places this year. He wants to describe all of them. Help Max finish his work. Read each paragraph. Then, write two more sentences describing the place. Use what Max tells you and what you already know to write the new sentences.

(1) In the fall, I went to the park. I saw children on swings and slides and three women sitting on a bench. I saw a boy walk towards the pond carrying a bag of bread.

_____

_____

(2) I went to the beach in the fall, too. Big waves of water rolled in and slapped the sand. I walked along the water's edge, and I saw empty shells and smooth stones.

_____

_____

(3) I went to the lake in the winter. I saw benches filled with people putting on ice skates. A man was selling hot chocolate at a small booth.

_____

_____

(4) I visited the aquarium this winter. I saw small tanks, big tanks, and giant-sized tanks! In one small tank, I saw sea horses. There was even a tank with a walking tunnel built into it. I walked in and looked up. Sharks swam over my head!

_____

_____

Directions: Figuring Out What Happens Next

Individual ●

Reproduce What Next? on page 34 for each student. Read the directions with the class. Then, have students work independently to complete the activity. Remind students to use what they see in the picture plus what they already know to decide or infer what the character in the picture will do next. Discuss the answers as a class.

Small Group ● ●

Divide the class into small groups of three or four students. Distribute one copy of What Next? to each group. Tell each group to select and cut out one of the pictures. Have each group fold a piece of construction paper in half and number the sides one and two. Have students glue the cut out picture on the first half. Next, have students work cooperatively to draw the second panel showing what happens next. Then, have students write a caption under each picture explaining what is happening. Display the results in class.

Collect and review the papers. Note the details in the "after" panel. Look for evidence of inference in the captions. Listen to the group discussions and encourage everyone to participate.

Whole Class ● ● ●

Reproduce What Next? on a transparency. Display the first illustration. Ask students what they know about the girl in the illustration. Lead the discussion with question prompts, such as, "What is she wearing? Where is she?" Record the students' answers and ask them to explain their answers.

Divide the class into two or three groups. Display the second illustration. Have students work with their group listing ideas about the character in the illustration. Later, have groups share and compare their lists. Discuss why the lists might not be the same.

What Next?

Directions: Look at each picture. Circle the letter before the correct answer. Then, write how you know the answer on the line.

1

What will the girl do next?

a) go skiing
b) go sledding
c) take off her boot
d) go to sleep

How do you know?

_____
_____

2

What will the girl do next?

a) play the violin
b) listen to music
c) take a walk
d) paint a picture

How do you know?

_____
_____

3

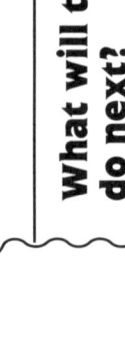

What will the boy do next?

a) climb down the ladder
b) dive into the pool
c) feed the birds
d) change his clothes

How do you know?

_____
_____

4

What will the boy do next?

a) walk home
b) play football
c) call a friend
d) ride the bike

How do you know?

_____
_____

Name: _____

Directions: Reading for Relationships

Individual

Reproduce Independent Reading 1 and 2 on pages 36 and 37 for each student. Read the directions with the class. Then, have students work independently to read each passage and answer the question. Have them underline the clues in the text that help them figure out the relationship. Remind students to use clues from the text plus what they already know to infer the relationship between the characters. Collect and review the papers.

Whole Class

Divide the class into groups of six. Explain that each group will work together to write three to five clues pointing to a relationship. Model the process. Think aloud, "If I want to let someone know two people were neighbors I might start with, 'In the summer, at night, Pam and I would sit by our bedroom windows and whisper across the alley to each other.' Then I would add, 'In the daytime, we sat on our porches talking into and listening through paper cups tied together by a long string.' For my third clue, 'We always drew a hopscotch board half in front of my house and half in front of hers so it would belong to both of us.'" Then, ask students if they think you and Pam were sisters, cousins, neighbors, or classmates.

On the board, write the following list: two cousins; two sisters; a parent and child; a grandparent and grandchild; a teacher and student; two friends. Tell groups of students to work together to make a list of three to five clues for each of the relationships. When they have finished, have groups share their lists with the class, while the other groups try to determine the relationship.

Small Group

Divide the class into pairs of students. Have each student write a paragraph describing his or her relationship with a family member, friend, classmate, or teacher, without saying who the person is in the text. Then, have students exchange paragraphs and guess who they are written about. Tell students to underline any clues that tell them who the people are.

Answer Key

Independent Reading 1 (Page 36)
1. b
2. d

Independent Reading 2 (Page 37)
1. d
2. a

Independent Reading 1

Directions: Read each story. Then, answer the question.

The boys looked at the garage floor, which was covered with toys. There wasn't enough space to park a bike. There was no way a car would fit in there. "This is a big job," Luis said. "Let's break it into smaller steps, so it's easier to tackle."

Marcos agreed. "That's a good idea. Let's start with the baseball gear."

Luis hung a long green bag on a hook on the garage wall. The boys filled it with bats, balls, and gloves. Next, they took out a plastic box and filled it with footballs and helmets. The boys continued sorting and storing the toys. After about an hour, Marcos said, "We still have a lot of work to do, and Mom said we have to finish by lunchtime."

Luis looked at his watch. "You're right," he said. "Mom said she would send Dad out at noon to check our work."

The boys went back to work. Finally, they saw nothing on the garage floor except their shadows. "Done!" Marcos shouted. "Now, there is plenty of room in here for a car."

Luis said, "Plus, now I know where to find my glove for my next game!"

 What word best describes Luis and Marcos?
   a) friends   c) teammates
   b) brothers   d) classmates

Thomas placed his hands on the keyboard. He knew this was Miss Laine's favorite song. He wanted each note to be perfect. He played the first few bars without a single mistake, and then he lost his place.

"You are doing a good job," Miss Laine said. "This is a tricky part." She showed Thomas how to play the next bar. Then, she tapped the music sheet with her pencil eraser and said, "Start from the beginning. I'll point to the notes, so you won't lose your place or rush through the music."

Thomas began the song again. He followed Miss Laine's pencil from note to note. He was surprised at how much it helped him keep time. When he finished the song, Thomas felt proud of his playing. He could tell Miss Laine was proud of him, too.

 What best describes Thomas and Miss Laine?
   a) friends   c) brother and sister
   b) strangers   d) student and teacher

Independent Reading 2

Directions: Read each story. Then answer the questions.

Sophie took a deep breath. The sweet smell of the cookies cooling on the counter filled her nose. "Did Mom help you make cookies when she was my age?" Sophie asked.

Nan nodded and pulled a book from a shelf. She opened the book and flipped through pages of photos. Nan tapped a picture. "This is your mother and me baking together," she said.

Sophie looked at the picture. "Didn't Aunt Julie bake with you, too?" she asked.

Nan turned the page and pointed at another photo. "Here is a picture of your mom, aunt, and grandfather eating the cookies. Your Aunt Julie always liked eating the cookies more than she liked baking!"

 What best describes Sophie and Nan?
a) sisters
b) cousins
c) daughter and mother
d) granddaughter and grandmother

Tim tossed and turned in bed. Tomorrow would be the first day of the family vacation. Tim looked forward to this all year. He was too excited to sleep!

Tim remembered when Mom said he could invite someone to come along. He knew who he wanted to ask right away. He and Jeff had met in preschool. They had done everything together since then. He knew Jeff would have a great time. When Jeff heard the news, he seemed as excited as Tim. The boys spent many days planning what to do on the trip.

Tim wondered if Jeff was asleep at his house. Maybe he was awake and thinking about the trip, too.

 What best describes Tim and Jeff?
a) friends
b) brothers
c) cousins
d) neighbors

Directions: Inferring Information

Individual ⚪

Reproduce "The Perfect Place" and "The Perfect Place" Questions on pages 39 and 40 for each student. Explain to the class that they will use the information in the graph and passage, plus what they already know, to infer the answer to each question. When all students have finished, ask them to share their answers with the class. Discuss what information in the graph or text helped them know the correct answer. Repeat the process with "Green School Fairs" on pages 41 and 42.

Whole Class ⚫⚫⚫

Reproduce "The Perfect Place" and "Green School Fairs" on transparencies. Divide the class into two teams. Display "The Perfect Place" graph/story, and read the story out loud. Then, read the first question associated with it and model the inference process. Think aloud, "I see by looking at the graph that Sue spent time watching different wild animals, but she also took time to drink lemonade and eat lunch. In the text, it says they walked through gates and from area to area. It also says she saw a map. I know when I go to a zoo there is usually a map, a gate, and different animals in different areas. So putting together the clues from the graph and the story with what I already know gives me the idea that Sue and her dad went to the zoo."

Have one student from each team stand. Ask the second question aloud. The first standing student to answer correctly scores two points for his or her team. As the question is asked, have other team members record the question number and answer on a separate sheet of paper. After the standing student answers, ask how many students agree with the answer. Then, the student standing for the other team can earn his or her team one point by stating the information used to infer the answer and where the information was found (graph, text, or both). Continue the process, rotating standing students. Repeat with the second graph set.

Answer Key

"The Perfect Place" Questions (Page 40)	"Green School Fairs" Questions (Page 42)
1. a	1. b
2. d	2. a
3. c	3. c
4. b	4. d
5. d	5. b
6. c	6. a

The Perfect Place

Sue told her dad about the book she read. When she finished, she said, "I thought I wanted to work with you when I grow up. Keeping pets healthy is an important job. Then I read this book. Now, I think I want to work with something bigger than a cat or dog."

Dad said, "Since you liked the book so much, I know where we should go tomorrow. It will be a surprise for you."

The next morning, Sue dressed in a T-shirt, shorts, and sneakers. She looked out the window and then grabbed her sunglasses. After breakfast, Sue and her dad boarded a bus. When they got off, Sue saw a sign with a picture of a monkey on it. Her dad bought tickets, and they went inside the gates. Sue saw a big map. She looked at it and picked out the areas she wanted to visit.

After a couple of hours, they sat on a bench and drank lemonade. Then, Sue was ready to see more. They walked along the path. Sue noticed that many people were looking in some areas, but other areas were empty. Finally, Dad said, "I'm hungry. Let's eat!"

Sue and Dad sat at a table in front of a food stand. When they finished eating, Dad pointed at clouds building in the sky. "It looks like the weather may change soon. Let's go home, and we can come back next week to see more," Dad said.

"This was the perfect place to come to today," said Sue. "And that sounds like the perfect plan."

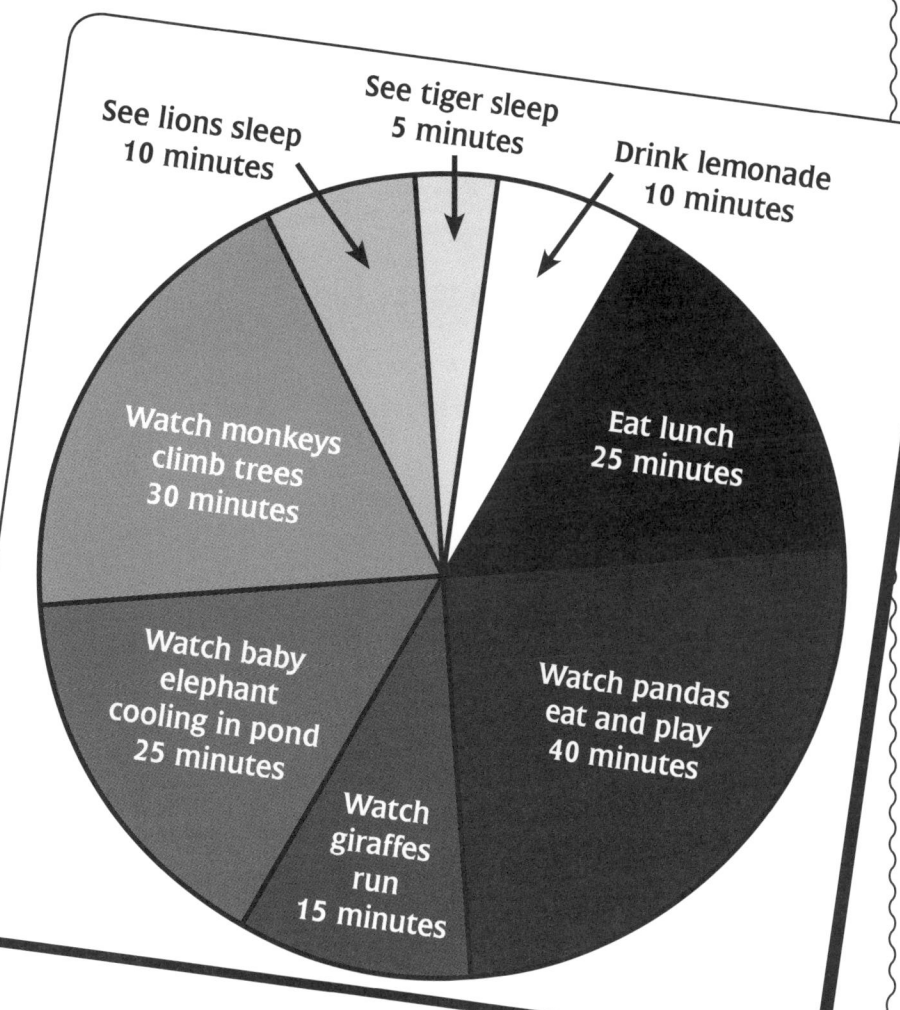

Name:_____

Directions: Use the graph and the story to answer the questions.

1 **Where did Sue and Dad visit?**
   a) zoo
   b) farm
   c) library
   d) museum

2 **What was Sue's book about?**
   a) maps
   b) buses
   c) fathers
   d) animals

3 **What animal did Sue most like to watch?**
   a) lion
   b) tiger
   c) panda
   d) giraffe

4 **What best describes the weather for Sue's trip?**
   a) hot and rainy
   b) hot and sunny
   c) cool and rainy
   d) cool and sunny

5 **What is Dad's job?**
   a) bus driver
   b) zoo keeper
   c) book author
   d) animal doctor

6 **Sue would agree that:**
   a) Too many people spend time watching the pandas play.
   b) Children should always do the same jobs as their parents.
   c) It is more fun to watch animals play than to watch them sleep.
   d) Being a zookeeper is more important than being an animal doctor.

Green School Fairs

Green School holds two student fairs each school year. This year, the second grade helped in November. They sold tickets for food, drinks, and events at the Give Thanks Fair. In June, the third grade helped. They sold the tickets for the Flag Day Fair. The graph shows what each grade sold.

■ = 2nd grade   ▨ = 3rd grade

"Green School Fairs" Questions

Directions: Use the "Green School Fairs" graph to answer the questions.

1 **What was the weather for the Flag Day Fair?**

a) hot and rainy

b) hot and sunny

c) cold and rainy

d) cold and sunny

2 **What do you think people wore to the Give Thanks Fair?**

a) warm coats

b) bathing suits

c) shorts

d) sandals

3 **Why didn't the third grade students sell any hot chocolate?**

a) They are too young to sell hot drinks.

b) No one at Green School likes chocolate.

c) It was too warm for a hot drink.

d) No one at the fair was thirsty.

4 **What event most likely was the most popular at the Give Thanks Fair?**

a) the water balloon race on the football field

b) the bicycle race in the parking lot

c) the scarecrow contest on the playground

d) the riddle contest in the library

5 **What other food most likely would have sold well at the Flag Day Fair?**

a) hot chili

b) ice pops

c) hot turkey sandwich

d) vegetable soup

6 **Why did the second grade sell more chicken soup than the third grade?**

a) It was cold out in November.

b) They are better salespeople.

c) Everyone likes chicken soup.

d) They had nothing else to sell.

Directions: In the News

Individual ●

Reproduce "The Nose Knows" and "Students and Parents Team Up to Go Green" articles and questions on pages 44–47 for each student. Have students read the articles and answer the questions independently. Ask students to highlight or underline the information in the articles that helped them answer the questions. Remind students they will need to put together information in the articles and what they already know to infer the correct answer. Collect and review the papers.

Small Group ● ●

Break the class into groups of three or four students. Reproduce the articles "The Nose Knows" and "Students and Parents Team Up to Go Green," and distribute one set of articles per group. Reproduce the Who, What, When, Where, and Why Graphic Organizer on page 48 for each group. Read the first article with the class. Tell students they will use their charts to collect information and ideas from the article. Give the students an example. On the board, write the five headings. Under "Who" write: "The dogs wear bright green jackets. The dogs must be easy to spot." Have each group fill in each section they are able to on their chart. Have students review their lists under each heading and underline the things they know because they used clues in the text. Have groups share their findings with the class. Repeat the process with the second article. Collect and review the papers. Listen to the students' explanations of the answers.

Answer Key

"The Nose Knows" Questions (Page 45)	"Team Up to Go Green" Questions (Page 47)
1. c	1. b
2. d	2. c
3. c	3. d
4. b	4. a
5. a	5. a
6. a	6. d

The Nose Knows

The United States Department of Agriculture (USDA) has a group of very special workers. They are short. They are cute. They are furry and have four legs! People call them the Beagle Brigade.

Why Beagles?

Beagles have a great sense of smell. They have about 44 times more smelling cells than people have. They are also very smart. The dogs can learn about 50 scents. They can tell one scent from another. This is very important for the job they do. Beagles are also small and friendly. Since they often work around large groups of people, this is important.

What Do They Do?

Some plants and meats carry pests and sickness. The United States has laws to keep these things out of the country. The beagles train to smell these fruits and vegetables. They learn how to smell the meats and plants by working with human partners. The pairs work in airports, in ship ports, and at land borders. Some teams even work in post offices. The dogs, wearing bright green jackets, sniff people's bags when they come into the country. Sometimes a dog smells a forbidden plant or food. Then, it sits down next to the bag. The dog's partner talks to the bag's owner and then looks inside the bag.

The beagles are right most of the time. After about two years on the job, they are right nine out of 10 times. Each year they catch about 75,000 unwanted plants and foods. This is a big help to farmers trying to grow healthy crops.

Making the Grade

Not all beagles are right for the Beagle Brigade. A vet clears each hopeful dog. Then, the dog trains for months. In the end, the dog's personality can make the difference between passing and failing. Some beagles are too friendly. Others are too shy. Still others don't have the energy to do the job well.

The good news is even if they don't make good work dogs, they still make great pets. When a dog leaves the program, a family welcomes it into their home.

"The Nose Knows" Questions

Name:_____

Directions: Circle the letter of the correct answer for each question.

1 **Most of the unwanted plants and foods come from _____.**

a) local farms

b) airport stores

c) other countries

d) the United States

2 **Why are the foods unwanted?**

a) They don't taste good.

b) They cost too much money.

c) They take up too much room in the bags.

d) They can pass pests to other plants and animals.

3 **Why does the program use small dogs?**

a) They fit inside the bags.

b) People won't see them.

c) People aren't afraid of them.

d) They can often work alone.

4 **Why are dogs turned down for being too friendly?**

a) The dogs would get along with their partners too well.

b) They might pay more attention to the people than the job.

c) People would not let them sniff their bags.

d) Too many families would want them for pets.

5 **Why would a beagle team work in a post office?**

a) Plants and foods might be mailed from other countries.

b) Beagles can also be trained to smell stamps and letters.

c) Someone can mail a beagle to another country to work.

d) The beagle might not work well around many strangers.

6 **Why are the dogs important to the USDA?**

a) They smell things people might not see.

b) They make airports friendlier places.

c) They are great pets for their partners.

d) They eat the bad plants and foods.

☆ The Daily News ☆

Students and Parents Team Up to Go Green

It all started with a book. Third grade teacher Kelly Jones read *Many Hands, One Goal* to her class. The book, by author Ida Wright, got Ms. Jones's students thinking. If the children in the book could make such an important change, why couldn't they do it too?

"The idea for the project came from a student," said Ms. Jones. "Jack wanted us to do this for the city."

The third grade students went right to work. They drew pictures of what the lot could look like. They read books about plants. They learned some trees, like orange trees, would not grow in the area. The winter months would be too hard on them. They learned some plants like lots of sun and some plants like lots of shade.

"When I saw how excited my students were, I knew this had to go further than drawing pictures," Ms. Jones said. She went to the Center School principal and asked for permission to turn the class's ideas into actions. "At first, Mr. Smith was not sold on the idea. Then, I told him about the science, math, social studies, and English lessons the students would learn from the project. That changed his mind."

So the students got to work. They wrote letters to the mayor asking for permission. They also wrote letters to their parents asking for help. They even wrote letters to garden stores in town. Then, they went to work on the lot. Students and parents cleaned the lot first. Once the trash was gone, they measured the land. Then, they started planting. One store donated two park benches. Another store gave them some trees. A third store gave plants and grass seed. Before long, the empty lot was a beautiful park.

The students knew their work was not done. They broke into teams. Two Saturdays every month, a team goes to the park to clean and weed. Most months they plant something new. The students learned they could not plant in January, February, or March. The ground was frozen. In April, they began planting spring and summer flowers.

The hard work has paid off. Many people enjoy the Main Street Park. It pulls more people onto Main Street. Store owners and shoppers love it. Most days you will see shoppers resting on benches in the park. So what's next? As one student said, "I hope people read our story and want to clean up a place near them."

"Team Up to Go Green" Questions

Name:_____

Directions: Circle the letter before the correct answer for each question.

1 **What kind of weather does the city have in winter?**

a) hot

b) cold

c) warm

d) cool

2 **What most likely was the book Many Hands, One Goal about?**

a) Center School

b) teaching the third grade

c) students making a difference

d) teams learning to play soccer

3 **Why didn't the principal like the idea at first?**

a) He doesn't like trees.

b) He didn't want to clean.

c) He did not want to pay for the plants and benches.

d) He did not know students could learn from the project.

4 **Why do you think the store owners love the park?**

a) It makes their customers happy.

b) People go to the park instead of the stores.

c) They sell the flowers that grow in the park.

d) It gives them more work to do outside.

5 **Why didn't the students plant during January, February, and March?**

a) The ground was too hard to dig into.

b) The park project ended in December.

c) People don't like to see flowers in the winter.

d) There were not enough teams to work then.

6 **What did the parents think about the park idea?**

a) It was silly.

b) It could not be done.

c) It cost too much money.

d) It was great.

Who, What, When, Where, and Why Graphic Organizer

Name:_____

Who?

What?

Where?

When?

Why?